# QUOTES FOR ALL OCCASIONS

ZUBIN GENIUSTRAINERS

ISBN 979-888591320-1

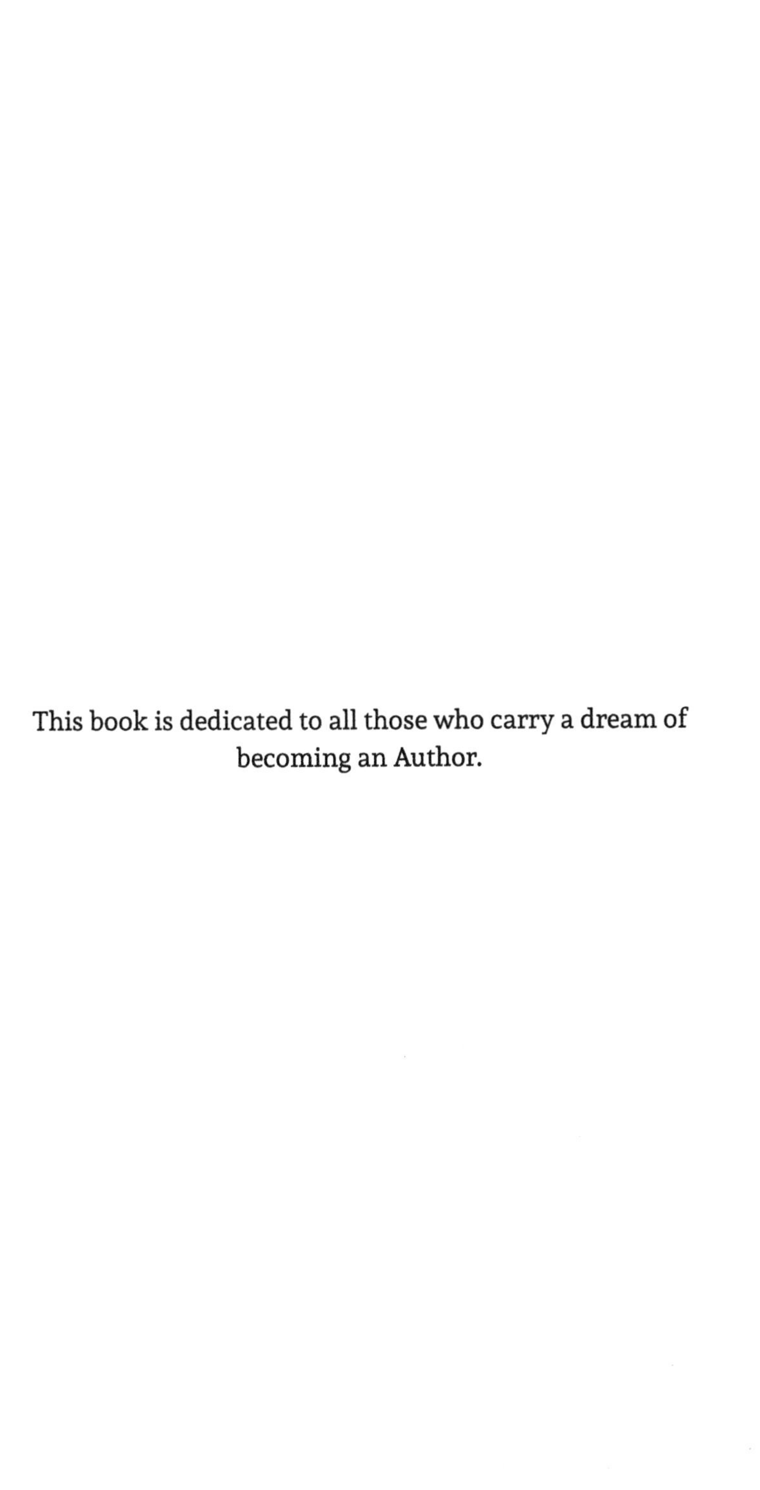

This book is dedicated to all those who carry a dream of becoming an Author.

# Contents

# Preface

This is a digital era and there are many struggling to fit in. Many of the so called old generation thinks that anything that involves technology is too complex. Being a trainer I have developed few trainings to support the so called old gen with the new technology. One such training is Be An Author in 7 Days where I train participants to publish their kindle book in just 7 days. Sometime the participants need a bit encouragement to believe that it is possible to create a book in 7 days. So I decided to show participants by publishing a book withing few hours and this is the result. This is a compilation of various quotes and you may find this a useful one.

# 1

# Acceptance, Tolerance & Taking a Stand

Acceptance

Tolerance implies no lack of commitment to one's own beliefs. Rather it condemns the oppression or persecution of others.
- John F. Kennedy

If civilization is to survive, we must cultivate the science of human relationships - the ability of all peoples, of all kinds, to live together, in the same world at peace.
- Franklin D. Roosevelt

Don't get so tolerant that you tolerate intolerance.
- Bill Maher

Be tolerant with others and strict with yourself.
- Marcus Aurelius

Intolerance is violence to the intellect and hatred is violence to the heart.
- Mahatma Gandhi

I have seen great intolerance shown in support of tolerance.
- Samuel Taylor Coleridge

Be more humble than a blade of grass, more tolerant than a tree, always offering respect onto others and never expecting any in return.
- Chaitanya Mahaprabhu

Compassion and tolerance are not a sign of weakness, but a sign of strength.
- Dalai Lama

Tolerance isn't about not having beliefs. It's about how your beliefs lead you to treat people who disagree with you.
- Timothy Keller

The test of courage comes when we are in the minority. The test of tolerance comes when we are in the majority.
- Ralph Washington Sockman

The responsibility of tolerance lies with those who have the wider vision.
- George Eliot

When traveling with someone, take large does of patience and tolerance with your morning coffee.
- Helen Hayes

Tolerance is held to be a condition of mind which is encouraged by, and is necessary for, civilization.

- Arthur Keith

It is thus tolerance that is the source of peace, and intolerance that is the source of disorder and squabbling.

- Pierre Bayle

The greatest gift that you can give to others is the gift of unconditional love and acceptance.

- Brian Tracy

Peace and justice are two sides of the same coin.

- Dwight D. Eisenhower

All blame is a waste of time. No matter how much fault you find with another, it will not change you.

- Wayne Dyer

Accepting others' life choices is something most people only learn with age.

- Neil Strauss

Darkness cannot drive out darkness; only light can do that. Hate cannot drive out hate; only love can do that.

- Martin Luther King, Jr.

There are two ways of exerting one's strength: one is pushing down, the other is pulling up.

- Booker T. Washington

Never doubt that a small group of thoughtful, committed citizens can change the world; indeed, it's the only thing that ever has.

- Margaret Mead

Social justice cannot be attained by violence. Violence kills what it intends to create.

- Pope John Paul II

Whatever affects one directly affects all indirectly.

- Martin Luther King, Jr.

Peace, however, is not merely a gift to be received: it is also a task to be undertaken.
- Pope Benedict XVI

I hate injustice, I despise inequity, I condemn hypocrisy, I abhor the lack of reason.
- Alexander Theroux

Suspicions which may be unjust need not be stated.
- Abraham Lincoln

When men no longer have the least fear of saying something untrue, they very soon have no fear whatsoever of doing something unjust.
- Theodor Haecker

Justice will not be served until those who are unaffected are as outraged as those who are.
- Benjamin Franklin

Be sure you put your feet in the right place, then stand firm.
- Abraham Lincoln

The man who stands firm in order to protect a sand-castle can never be relied upon; for he has given away his common sense.
- Winston Churchill

# 2

# Changing Attitude, Mindset & Improving Time Management

Time

If you don't like something, change it. If you can't change it, change your attitude.
- Maya Angelou

Man can alter his life by altering his thinking.
- William James

The greatest discovery of my generation is that a human being can alter his life by altering his attitudes.
- William James

When you're in conflict with someone, one factor can make the difference between damaging your relationship and deepening it. That factor is attitude.
- William James

Those who can't change their minds can't change anything.
- George Bernard Shaw

They always say time changes things, but you actually have to change them yourself.
- Andy Warhol

The most significant change in a person's life is a change of attitude.
- William J. Johnston

Your attitude, not your aptitude, will determine your altitude.
- Zig Ziglar

If you want to change attitudes, start with a change in behavior. In other words, begin to act the part.
- William Glasser

The only thing we can do is play on the one string we have, and that is our attitude.
- Charles R. Swindoll

Everyone thinks of changing the world, but no one thinks of changing himself.
- Leo Tolstoy

By changing our mindset and habits, we can actually dramatically change the course of life.

- Shawn Achor

All that we are is the result of what we have thought; what we think we become.

- Gautama Buddha

If you focus on results, you will never change. If you focus on change, you will get results.

- Jack Dixon

Only the wisest and stupidest of men never change.

- Confucius

As long as you manage your time properly, you can get everything done.

- John Cena

Being successful doesn't make you manage your time well. Managing your time well makes you successful!

- Randy Pausch

The key is not to prioritize what's on your schedule, but to schedule your priorities.

- Stephen Covey

If you look to lead, invest at least 40% of your time managing yourself

- your ethics, character, principles, purpose, motivation, and conduct.

- Dee Hock

Invest at least 30% of your time managing those with authority over you and 15% managing your peers.

- Dee Hock

No one has more time than you have. It is the discipline and stewardship of your time that is important.

- Jill Briscoe

The management of time is the management of self.

- Jill Briscoe

You can't manage time, you actually only manage what you do during time.
- David Allen

Time management is about how you manage your focus, actions and activities
- David Allen

There is nothing so useless as doing efficiently that which should not be done at all.
- Peter Drucker

I must govern the clock, not be governed by it.
- Golda Meir

Think of your priorities not in terms of what activities you do, but when you do them. Timing is everything.
- Dan Millman

There cannot be a crisis next week. My schedule is already full.
- Henry A. Kissinger

A schedule defends from chaos and whim. A net for catching days.
- Annie Dillard

I have a hard time with scheduling, and with hunkering down and planning. That's always been a struggle for me.
- Zachary Levi

I don't think that scheduling is uncreative. I think that structure is required for creativity.
- Twyla Tharp

# 3

# Embrace Love and Boost Self-Knowledge

Love

Your task is not to seek for love, but merely to seek and find all the barriers within yourself that you have built against it.
- Rumi

We are each of us angels with only one wing, and we can only fly by embracing one another.
- Luciano De Crescenzo

Life is short. Kiss slowly, laugh insanely, love truly and forgive quickly
- Paulo Coelho

To love someone is nothing, to be loved by someone is something, to love someone who loves you is everything.
- Bill Russell

A woman's heart should be so hidden in God that a man has to seek Him just to find her.
- Max Lucado

If you judge people, you have no time to love them.
- Mother Teresa

We come to love, not by finding the perfect person, but by learning to see an imperfect person perfectly.
- Sam Keen

When you love someone, you love the person as they are, and not as you'd like them to be.
- Leo Tolstoy

Being deeply loved by someone gives you strength, while loving someone deeply gives you courage.
- Laozi

Don't waste your love on somebody, who doesn't value it.
- William Shakespeare

You know it's love when all you want is that person to be happy, even if you're not part of their happiness.
- Julia Roberts

The consciousness, of loving and being loved, brings a warmth and richness to life that nothing else can bring.
- Oscar Wilde

A loving heart is the beginning of all knowledge.
- Thomas Carlyle

The best relationship is one in which your love for each other exceeds your need for each other.

- Dalai Lama

Beginnings are usually scary and endings are usually sad; but it's everything in between that makes it all worth living.

- Bob Marley

The one self- knowledge worth having is to know one's own mind.

- F. H. Bradley

Who looks outside, dreams; who looks inside, awakes.

- Carl Jung

If most of us remain ignorant of ourselves, it is because self-knowledge is painful and we prefer the pleasures of illusion.

- Aldous Huxley

Everything that irritates us about others can lead us to an understanding of ourselves.

- Carl Jung

All types of knowledge ultimately mean self-knowledge.

- Bruce Lee

Self-reverence, self-knowledge, self-control; these three alone lead one to sovereign power.

- Alfred Lord Tennyson

Freedom is knowing who you really are.

- Bill Vaughan

I want, by understanding myself, to understand others.

- Katherine Mansfield

Make it thy business to know thyself, which is the most difficult lesson in the world.

- Miguel de Cervantes

Knowing yourself is the beginning of all wisdom.

- Aristotle

Self-knowledge comes from knowing other men.
- von Goethe

It's not only the most difficult thing to know one's self, but the most inconvenient.
- Josh Billings

There are three things extremely hard: steel, a diamond, and to know one's self.
- Benjamin Franklin

One secures the gold of the spirit when he finds himself.
- Claude M. Bristol

Explore thyself. Herein are demanded the eye and the nerve.
- Henry David Thoreau

# 4

# Facing Your Fears & Learning to Be Happy

Happy

If you want to conquer fear, don't sit home and think about it. Go out and get busy.
- Dale Carnegie

You gain strength, courage, and confidence by every experience in which you really stop to look fear in the face.

You are able to say to yourself, 'I lived through this horror. I can take the next thing that comes along.'
- Eleanor Roosevelt

Don't let fear or insecurity stop you from trying new things. Believe in yourself. Do what you love. And most importantly, be kind to others, even if you don't like them.
- Stacy London

I've learned that fear limits you and your vision. It serves as blinders to what may be just a few steps down the road for you. The journey is valuable, but believing in your talents, your abilities, and your self-worth can empower you to walk down an even brighter path. Transforming fear into freedom - how great is that?
- Soledad O'Brien

Courage is resistance to fear, mastery of fear, not absence of fear.
- Mark Twain

Fear keeps us focused on the past or worried about the future. If we can acknowledge our fear, we can realize that right now we are okay. Right now, today, we are still alive, and our bodies are working marvelously. Our eyes can still see the beautiful sky. Our ears can still hear the voices of our loved ones.
- Thich Nhat Hanh

Some days, 24 hours is too much to stay put in, so I take the day hour by hour, moment by moment. I break the task, the challenge, the fear into small, bite-size pieces. I can handle a piece of fear, depression, anger, pain, sadness, loneliness, illness. I actually put my hands up to my face, one next to each eye, like blinders on a horse.
- Regina Brett

You always have two choices: your commitment versus your fear.

- Sammy Davis, Jr.

Limits, like fear, is often an illusion.

- Michael Jordan

My story is a freedom song of struggle. It is about finding one's purpose, how to overcome fear and to stand up for causes bigger than one's self.

- Coretta Scott King

Living with fear stops us taking risks, and if you don't go out on the branch, you're never going to get the best fruit.

- Sarah Parish

Remembering that I'll be dead soon is the most important tool I've ever encountered to help me make the big choices in life. Because almost everything - all external expectations, all pride, all fear of embarrassment or failure- these things just fall away in the face of death, leaving only what is truly important.

- Steve Jobs

You just have to get rid of fear and confront the world. Look at yourself in the mirror and say to yourself, 'I love you and nothing will destroy you and you're not going to fall.'

- Ricky Martin

Have no fear of perfection - you'll never reach it.

- Salvador Dali

My motto is: feel the fear and do it anyway.

- Tamara Mellon

You don't develop courage by being happy in your relationships every day. You develop it by surviving difficult times and challenging adversity. -Epicurus

There are two ways of being happy: We must either diminish our wants or augment our means – either may do – the result is the same and it is for each man to decide for himself and to do that which happens to be easier.

- - Benjamin Franklin

Success is not the key to happiness. Happiness is the key to success. If you love what you are doing, you will be successful.
- Albert Schweitzer

No one is in control of your happiness but you; therefore, you have the power to change anything about yourself or your life that you want to change.
- Barbara DeAngelis

Too often in life, something happens, and we blame other people for us not being happy or satisfied or fulfilled. So, the point is, we all have choices, and we make the choice to accept people or situations or to not accept situations.
- Tom Brady

The habit of being happy enables one to be freed, or largely freed, from the domination of outward conditions.
– Robert Louis Stevenson

A truly happy person is one who can enjoy the scenery while on a detour.
– Author Unknown

We tend to forget that happiness doesn't come as a result of getting something we don't have, but rather of recognizing and appreciating what we do have.
- Frederick Keonig

Happiness is not a station you arrive at, but a manner of traveling.
- Margaret Lee Runbeck

True happiness is not attained through self-gratification, but through fidelity to a worthy purpose.
- Helen Keller

Most of us are just about as happy as we make up our minds to be.
- William Adams

Look at everything as though you were seeing it either for the first or last time. Then your time on earth will be filled with glory.

- Betty Smith

You are the one that possesses the keys to your being. You carry the passport to your own happiness.

- Diane von Furstenberg

Do things that make you happy within the confines of the legally system. Seriously. I'm Kidding.

– Ellen DeGeneres

You need to learn how to select your thoughts just the same way you select your clothes every day. This is a power you can cultivate.

– Elizabeth Gilbert

# 5

# Gratitude Towards Others & Relaxation Quotes

Gratitude

Gratitude is not only the greatest of virtues, but the parent of all the others.
- Marcus Tullius Cicero

At times, our own light is rekindled by a spark from another person. Each of us has cause to think with deep gratitude of those who have lighted the flame within us.

- Albert Schweitzer

Appreciation is a wonderful thing: It makes what is excellent in others belong to us as well.

- Voltaire

Feeling gratitude and not expressing it is like wrapping a present and not giving it.

- William Arthur Ward

No one who achieves success does so without acknowledging the help of others. The wise and confident acknowledge this help with gratitude.

- Alfred North Whitehead

Acknowledging the good that you already have in your life is the foundation for all abundance.

- Eckhart Tolle

Showing gratitude is one of the simplest yet most powerful things humans can do for each other.

- Randy Pausch

Let us be grateful to people who make us happy, they are the charming gardeners who make our souls blossom.

- Marcel Proust

As we express our gratitude, we must never forget that the highest appreciation is not to utter words, but to live by them.

- John F. Kennedy

I would maintain that thanks are the highest form of thought; and that gratitude is happiness doubled by wonder.

- Gilbert K. Chesterton

There is a calmness to a life lived in gratitude, a quiet joy.

- Ralph Blum

Gratitude turns what we have into enough.
- Melody Beattie

Truly appreciate those around you, and you'll find many others around you.
- Ralph Marston

Appreciation can make a day - even change a life.
- Margaret Cousins

Nothing is more honorable than a grateful heart.
- Seneca the Younger

Your mind will answer most questions if you learn to relax and wait for the answer.
- William S. Burroughs

The time to relax is when you don't have time for it.
- Sydney J. Harris

Each person deserves a day away in which no problems are confronted, no solutions searched for.
- Maya Angelou

Whenever in doubt, turn off your mind, relax, and float downstream.
- John Lennon

Learn to relax. Your body is precious, as it houses your mind and spirit. Inner peace begins with a relaxed body.
- Norman Vincent Peale

No matter how much pressure you feel at work, if you could find ways to relax for at least five minutes every hour, you'd be more productive.
- Joyce Brothers

Every now and then go away, have a little relaxation, for when you come back to your work your judgment will be surer.
- Leonardo da Vinci

Sometimes the most important thing in a whole day is the rest we take between two deep breaths or the turning inwards in prayer for five short minutes.

- Etty Hillesum

The only pressure I'm under is the pressure I've put on myself.

- Mark Messier

Try to relax and enjoy the crisis.

- Ashleigh Brilliant

A crust eaten in peace is better than a banquet partaken in anxiety.

- Aesop

Doing something positive will help turn your mood around. When you smile, your body relaxes. When you experience human touch and interaction, it eases tension in your body.

- Simone Elkeles

Relax, ease back in your seat, and let the music take you wherever it does.

- John Denver

Show me a worrying person and I will show you a person who does not know how to relax.

- Albert E Cliffe

If people concentrated on the really important things in life, there'd be a shortage of fishing poles.

- Doug Larson

# 6

# Living Intensely & Loyalty

Loyalty

Your progress depends on your degree of sustained intensity in a given direction.
- Roger McDonald

Life is not just the passing of time. Life is the collection of experiences and their intensity.

- Jim Rohn

I approached everything, my job, my family, my romances, with intensity.

- Gene Tierney

Long-term consistency trumps short-term intensity.

- Bruce Lee

The trick is in what one emphasizes. We either make ourselves miserable or happy. The amount of work is the same.

- Carlos Castaneda

Do not try to do extraordinary things but do ordinary things with intensity.

- Emily Carr

Genius, by its very intensity, decrees a special path of fire for its vivid power.

- Phillips Brooks

Progress is measured by richness and intensity of experience.

- Herbert Read

Intense love does not measure, it just gives.

- Mother Teresa

The true warrior understands and seizes that moment by giving an effort so intense and so intuitive that it could only be called one from the heart.

- Pat Riley

Reflective thinking enables you to distance yourself from the intense emotions of particularly good or bad experiences and see them with fresh eyes.

- John C. Maxwell

Intense feeling too often obscures the truth.

- Harry S. Truman

I'm not sure which is worse: intense feeling, or the absence of it.

- Margaret Atwood

Survival is not possible if the best of us lack all conviction, while the worst of us are full of passionate intensity.

- John Silber

Try to live with the same intensity as a child. He doesn't ask for explanations; he dives into each day as if it were a new adventure and, at night, sleeps happy.

- Paulo Coelho

Never forget that friendship and loyalty are more precious than riches.

- Brian Jacques

The best gifts to give: To your friend, loyalty; To your enemy, forgiveness; To your boss, service; To a child, a good example.

- Oren Arnold

No two things are more valued in another person than trust and loyalty.

- Zig Ziglar

Loyalty embraces the best human characters: courage, faith, love, and charity.

- Douglas Bader

The secret of a good life is to have the right loyalties and hold them in the right scale of values.

- Norman Thomas

Lack of loyalty is one of the major causes of failure in every walk of life.

- Napoleon Hill

You don't earn loyalty in a day. You earn loyalty day-by-day.

- Jeffrey Gitomer

Loyalty means nothing unless it has at its heart the absolute principle of self-sacrifice.

- Woodrow Wilson

We are all in the same boat, in a stormy sea, and we owe each other a terrible loyalty.

- Gilbert K. Chesterton

Success rests not only on ability, but upon commitment, loyalty, and pride.

- Vince Lombardi

Loyalty to the country always. Loyalty to the government when it deserves it.

- Mark Twain

Without trust, there can be no loyalty and without loyalty, there can be no true growth.

- Fred Reichheld

The greater the loyalty of a group toward the group, the greater the motivation among the members to achieve its goals.

- Rensis Likert

I try to plant peace if I do not want discord; to plant loyalty and honesty if I want to avoid betrayal and lies.

- Maya Angelou

Loyalty is the pledge of truth to oneself and others.

- Ada Velez

# 7

# Overcoming Procrastination & Developing Social Relations

Procrastination

Incomplete tasks in your head consume the energy of your attention as they gnaw at your conscience.
- Brahma Kumaris

Folks who tell you, "Putting it off won't make it any easier," presume there's a point where you plan to stop putting it off.
- Robert Brault

Procrastination is the grave in which opportunity is buried.
- Alyce Cornyn-Selby

Avoiding problems you need to face is avoiding the life you need to live.
- Paulo Coelho

Avoidance allows you to believe that you're making all kinds of strides.
- Liz Murray

Things dreaded require double time to accomplish them.
- James Lendall Basford

Every duty which is bidden to wait returns with seven fresh duties at its back.
- Charles Kingsley

You may delay, but time will not.
- Benjamin Franklin

To think too long about doing a thing often becomes its undoing.
- Eva Young

Don't fool yourself that important things can be put off till tomorrow; they can be put off forever, or not at all.
- Mignon McLaughlin

To make an easy job seem mighty hard, just keep putting off doing it.
- Olin Miller

The best way to get something done is to begin.
- Unknown

You know you are getting old when it takes too much effort to procrastinate.
- Unknown

You don't have to see the whole staircase, just take the first step.
- MLK

You cannot escape the responsibility of tomorrow by evading it today.
- Abraham Lincoln

The best way to deal with procrastination is to postpone it.
- Tony Robbins

I don't wait for moods. You accomplish nothing if you do that. Your mind must know it has got to get down to work.
- Pearl S. Buck

To combat social awkwardness, I would just act like I couldn't be bothered - that kind of aloof persona or aloof demeanor. It's so off-putting.
- Janeane Garofalo

The fear of being laughed at makes cowards of us all.
- Mignon McLaughlin

The deepest principle in human nature is the craving to be appreciated.
- William James

We're losing social skills, the human interaction skills, how to read a person's mood, to read their body language, how to be patient until the moment is right.
- Vincent Nichols

Genuine relationships depend first on a healthy relationship with ourselves.
- Sonia Choquette

The best way to keep relationships happy, healthy, and supportive can be summed up in one word: appreciation.
- Marci Shimoff

Work on your relationships... Relationships need renewal or they die.
- Bo Sanchez

Keep your standards high, and any guy who is worth it will rise to meet them.
- Ed Westwick

The only way a relationship will last is if you see it as a place that you go to give, and not a place that you go to take.
- Tony Robbins

In a relationship, you can either be right or happy. You'll soon find that you don't care that much about being right.
- Ralphie May

You can make more friends in two months by becoming interested in other people than you can in two years by trying to get other people interested in you.
- Dale Carnegie

A growing relationship can only be nurtured by genuineness.
- Leo Buscaglia

How happy you are depends to a very large degree on your relationships with other people.
- Zig Ziglar

It's not too late to develop new friendships or reconnect with people.
- Morrie Schwartz

Friends aren't jumper cables. You don't throw them into the trunk and pull them out for emergencies.
- Charlie Krueger

The language of friendship is not words but meanings.
- Henry David Thoreau

The only way to have a friend is to be one.
- Ralph Waldo Emerson

The best relationships, the ones that last, are the ones rooted in friendship.
- Gillian Anderson

# 8

# Personal Development

Personal Development

You cannot shake hands with a clenched fist.
- Indira Gandhi

Above all, be the heroine of your life, not the victim.
- Nora Ephron

Everything you are against weakens you. Everything you are for empowers you.
- Wayne Dyer

If you want something said, ask a man. If you want something done, ask a woman.
- Margaret Thatcher

I have learned over the years that when one's mind is made up, this diminishes fear; knowing what must be done does away with fear.
- Rosa Parks

Until you're ready to look foolish, you'll never have the possibility of being great.
- Cher

I no longer criticize anyone--not even myself. I only give out positive vibes.
- Louise Hay

Giving appreciation, praise, and gratitude feels good and puts good vibes in the environment.
- Jude Bijou

If you want to learn to trust your vibes, you must maintain a peaceful and relatively calm attitude.
- Sonia Choquette

Not trusting your sixth sense, will always come back to haunt you. Have the courage to stand alone and trust your vibes.
- Sonia Choquette

Once you replace negative thoughts with positive ones, you'll start having positive results.
- Willie Nelson

If you want to find the secrets of the universe, think in terms of energy, frequency, and vibration.
- Nikola Tesla

Reality is that which, when you stop believing in it, doesn't go away.
- Robert Collier

What we continually think about eventually will manifest in our lives.
- Robert Collier

A flow of happiness and abundance will manifest when you have reached the deepest level of yourself.
- Deepak Chopra

The thought manifests as the word. The word manifests as the deed. The deed develops into habit. And the habit hardens into character.
- Gautama Buddha

The visible is always a mirror of the invisible. The reality is imagined before it manifests itself.
- Paulo Coelho

Think positive thoughts, intensely. Grow enthusiastic images, boldly. Speak only wonderful words to yourself, constantly. Feel fantastic, NOW! This colors your view of the world. Like a magnet, you attract the resources necessary to manifest the world you desire.
- Mark Victor Hansen

Life is to be enjoyed, not just endured.
- Gordon B. Hinckley

Life is a self-fulfilling prophecy. What you believe about life will be your experience of life.
- Neale Donald Walsch

In the end, it's not the years in your life that count. It's the life in your years.
- Abraham Lincoln

Life is more fun and manageable when thought of as a scavenger hunt as opposed to a surprise party.
- Jimmy Buffett

Fill what is empty, empty what is full, and scratch where it itches.
- Tallulah Bankhead

Education provides the fullest opportunities for fulfilling ourselves. It is the access to all that a person has yet to learn.
- Lowell Milken

Fitness is an entry point to help you build a happier, healthier life.
- Jillian Michaels

The groundwork of all happiness is health.
- Leigh Hunt

Healthy habits are learned in the same way as unhealthy ones - through practice.
- Wayne Dyer

Take care of your body. It's the only place you have to live.
- Jim Rohn

The secret of health for mind and body is to live the present moment wisely and earnestly.
- Gautama Buddha

Laughter is an important part of healthy living.
- Matthew Moy

Living consciously involves being genuine; listening and responding to others honestly and openly. It involves being in the moment.
- Sidney Poitier

We can only be said to be alive in those moments when our hearts are conscious of our treasures.
- Thornton Wilder

A commitment to lifelong learning is a natural expression of the practice of living consciously.
- Nathaniel Branden

Life is about not knowing, having to change, taking the moment, and making the best of it, without knowing what's going to happen next.

- Gilda Radner

If you spend your whole life waiting for the storm, you'll never enjoy the sunshine.

- Morris West

The purpose of life is to live it, to taste experience to the utmost, to reach out eagerly and without fear for newer and richer experience.

- Eleanor Roosevelt

Visualization is daydreaming with a purpose.

- Bo Bennett

When you visualize, then you materialize.

- Denis Waitley

Begin by imagining the impossible and end by accomplishing the impossible.

- Sri Chinmoy

To bring anything into your life, imagine it's already there.

- Richard Bach

Visualize the thing you want. See it, feel it, believe in it. Make your mental blueprint and begin.

- Robert Collier

Logic will get you from A to B. Imagination will take you everywhere.

- Albert Einstein

You'll never find a better sparring partner than adversity.

- Golda Meir

Only those who dare to fail greatly can ever achieve greatly.

- Robert Kennedy

When you suffer a setback or disappointment, put your head down, and plow ahead.

- Les Brown

Victory is always possible for people who refuse to stop fighting.
- Napoleon Hill

Life's challenges shouldn't paralyze you. They should help you discover who you are.
- Bernice Johnson Reagon

Only those who will risk going too far can possibly find out how far one can go.
- T. S. Eliot

Don't find fault, find the remedy.
- Henry Ford.

Leaders who give their best get the best from others.
- Lee Colan

Outstanding leaders go out of their way to boost the self-esteem of their personnel.
- Sam Walton

The greatest leader isn't necessarily the one who does the greatest things. He is the one that gets the people to do the greatest things.
- Ronald Reagan

People buy into the leader before they buy into the vision.
- John Maxwell

Management is about arranging and telling. Leadership is about nurturing and enhancing.
- Tom Peters

Attitude is a small thing that makes a big difference.
- Winston Churchill

Don't fear starting over. You can build something better.
- Unknown

Act as if what you do makes a difference. It does.
- William James

When I do good, I feel good.

- Abraham Lincoln

The world is full of suffering; it is also full of the overcoming.

- Helen Keller

# 9

# Set Realistic Expectations & Change Circumstances

Expectation

Realistic expectations for life are that we are going to be better today than we were yesterday.
- Jim Harbaugh

Having realistic expectations about your day-to-day challenges are the keys to stress management, which is perhaps the most important ingredient to living a happy, healthy and rewarding life.

- Marilu Henner

Set realistic customer expectations and then not to just meet them, but to exceed them - preferably in unexpected and helpful ways.

- Richard Branson

Professional accountability is a good thing. Without it, excellence is merely a pipe dream and even average performance isn't a realistic expectation.

- Leon F. "Lee" Ellis

Rely on virtues that intelligent, balanced humans have relied on for centuries: common sense, thrift, realistic expectations, patience, and perseverance.

- John C. Bogle

A realistic expectation demands our acceptance that one's allotted time must be limited.

- Sherwin B. Nuland

If you do not expect the unexpected, you will not recognize it when it arrives.

- Heraclitus

Don't expect to build up the weak by pulling down the strong.

- Calvin Coolidge

Never idealize others. They will never live up to your expectations.

- Leo Buscaglia

I would like my car to fly and make me breakfast, but that's an unrealistic expectation.

- Jack Tretton

You have to find out what's right for you, so it's trial and error. You are going to be all right if you accept realistic goals for yourself.

- Teri Garr

The goal you set must be challenging. At the same time, it should be realistic and attainable, not impossible to reach. It should be challenging enough to make you stretch, but not so far that you break.

- Rick Hansen

What we need are positive, realistic goals and the willingness to work. Hard work and practical goals.

- Kareem Abdul-Jabbar

What we need are positive, realistic goals and the willingness to work hard.- Kareem Abdul-Jabbar

The journey begins with the contemplation stage of specifying realistic goals, getting ready, or getting psyched.

- John C. Norcross

You don't drown by falling in the water; you drown by staying there.

- Edwin Louis Cole

If I want to change my reality, then it is time for me to change my mind.

- Louise Hay

Your present circumstances don't determine where you can go; they merely determine where you start.

- Nido R Qubein

To hell with circumstances, I create opportunities.

- Bruce Lee

Extraordinary people survive under the most terrible circumstances and they become more extraordinary because of it.

- Robertson Davies

I am determined to be cheerful and happy in whatever situation I may find myself. For our misery or unhappiness is determined not by our circumstance but by our disposition.

- Martha Washington

Take personal responsibility. You cannot change the circumstances, the seasons, or the wind, but you can change yourself. That is something you have charge of.

- Jim Rohn

Men are anxious to improve their circumstances, but are unwilling to improve themselves; they therefore remain bound.

- James Allen

Wise men put their trust in ideas and not in circumstances.

- Ralph Waldo Emerson

Circumstances do not make the man, they reveal him.

- James Allen

Don't underestimate players or audiences in any circumstances.

- Peter Maxwell Davies

You may not seem able to change some outer circumstances but you can start by changing your inner experience of life and yourself.

- Joy Page

The function of intellect is to provide a means of modifying our reactions to the circumstances of life.

- Edward Thorndike

No change of circumstances can repair a defect of character.

- Ralph Waldo Emerson

Others' circumstances seem good to us and ours seem good to others.

- Publilius Syrus

# 10

# Tactful Communication & Improve Stamina

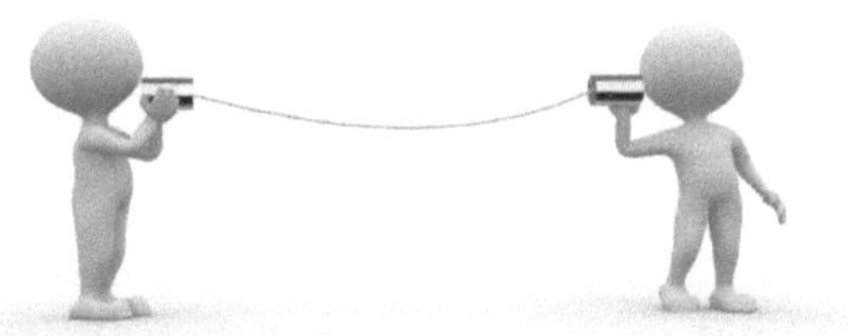

Communication

Tact is the ability to make a person see lightning without letting him feel the bolt.
- Orlando Aloysius Battista

Tact is the ability to describe others as they see themselves.

- Abraham Lincoln

Step with care and great tact. And remember life's a great balancing act.

- Dr. Seuss

Tact is the art of making a point without making an enemy.

- Isaac Newton

Tact is to lie about others as you would have them lie about you.

- Oliver Herford

Tact is the unsaid part of what you think.

- Henry Van Dyke

Because there can be consequences for saying the first thing that pops into our heads, it is prudent to exercise tact.

- Jeanne Phillips

Manners are a sensitive awareness of the feelings of others.

- Emily Post

Tact is rubbing out another's mistake instead of rubbing it in.

- Leo Buscaglia

Be sure, when you think you are being extremely tactful, that you are not in reality running away from something you ought to face.

- Frank Medlicott

The hardest job kids face today is learning good manners without seeing any.

- Fred Astaire

If there were one word that could act as a standard of conduct for one's entire life, perhaps it would be 'thoughtfulness.

- Confucius

Communication leads to community, that is, to understanding, intimacy and mutual valuing.
- Rollo May

If you just communicate, you can get by. But if you communicate skillfully, you can work miracles.
- Jim Rohn

Communication is a skill that you can learn. It's like riding a bicycle or typing. If you're willing to work at it, you can improve the quality of every part of your life.
- Brian Tracy

Human kindness has never weakened the stamina or softened the fiber of a free people. A nation does not have to be cruel to be tough.
- Franklin D. Roosevelt

How you start is important, but it is how you finish that counts. In the race for success, speed is less important than stamina.
- B. C. Forbes

To succeed, we must have the will to succeed; we must have stamina, determination, backbone, perseverance, self-reliance, and faith.
- B. C. Forbes

This is a stamina game, so don't despair if you run down a blind alley and have to start over.
- Tim Maleeny

Your effort and continued dedication distinguish you from those who don't have the courage or stamina to try.
- Daniel Klatt

If we didn't struggle through some things, we would never develop the strength and stamina we need to survive in this world.
- Joyce Meyer

In writing, as in medicine, there are no short cuts. You need stamina.
- Abraham Verghese

Fortitude is the guard and support of the other virtues.
- John Locke

In struggling with misfortunes lies the true proof of virtue.
- William Shakespeare

You mature as far as your understanding and you increase your stamina. You don't let frustration overtake you when you're looking for change.
- Eddie Vedder

The practice of being at ease also gives you the strength and stamina to pursue all that you find when you connect inward.
- Tara Stiles

All the world is full of suffering. It is also full of overcoming.
- Helen Keller

Endurance is patience concentrated.
- Thomas Carlyle

Man never made any material as resilient as the human spirit.
- Bernard Williams

Endurance is one of the most difficult disciplines but it is to the one who endures that the final victory comes.
- Gautama Buddha

9 798885 913201

Printed by Libri Plureos GmbH in Hamburg,
Germany